BERLIN – PAST, PRESENT AND FUTURE

We don't need any luggage to go on a trip through time – an exciting tour through six millennia! Experts date the first traces of human settlement in the area of Berlin back to somewhere around 4000 B.C. Farmers, tired of their dangerous nomadic existence, came here and joined forces to live more safely. A glance back in time can only throw a little light on how this area has changed and indeed was forced to change over the course of time. The Rivers Havel and Spree which meet here became important transportation channels three hundred years A.D. This was not only a place of work, booze and frivolity, it was also a centre of trade with guilds and a court. Fixed rules of play and solid prices. A market with rough Pagan ways and customs: an eye for an eye, a tooth for a tooth. The people had to wait 500 years for the Catholic belief. Only around 950 did Prince Otto I, whose administrative centre was still Brandenburg on the River Havel at that time, bring Christianity to the country. Another two hundred years later, Albrecht, the "Bear" paved the way for what we can now call a politically stable and strategically

◁ Unter den Linden around 1780

Berlin Panorama of the city ▽

important region from the stretch of land between the River Oder to the East and the River Elbe to the West: the Brandenburg March. We could use a more crude turn of phrase: This was the land of rough squires who were quite capable of putting the fear of God into their neighbours. Berlin and Coelln, its counterpart on the other shore of the Spree, attain such significance at the beginning of the 13th century that a merger of the two is a fore-gone conclusion. Berlin receives town rights in 1231. Only two generations later the ferrymen are a thing of the past and a bridge provides the link between the people on either side of the river. In 1307 the process is complete and the four guilds – clothmaker, shoemaker, butcher and baker – sign and seal the contract which allies finance, military and foreign policy. In 1411 the Royal Edict of Rimini confirms that a princely family from Franconia is to take over stately power: the Hohenzollerns. Three decades later the foundati-ons for a mighty castle are laid. Berlin as the new, the only residence. The political importance of the town and indeed its economic significance remains small, however. Elsewhere in Europe, other cities

▽ *Berlin · Panorama of the city by night*

such as the Hanseatic Ports, markets along the salt roads, global centres such as Paris, Madrid and Vienna have obtained such prominent positions that Berlin is seldom seen on the map. Frederick II finally manages to irrevocably put his capital on the continental map through three wars against Austria. One hundred years later William I is proclaimed German Kaiser in Versailles, marking the birth of the Reich in 1871. Prussia as a fearful factor of power from the very first hour. Tumultuous times are on the horizon; the population explodes in the metropolis as a consequence of the Gründerzeit boom. In 1912 four million people live in and around Berlin. The First World War punishes the Kaiser's abuse of power and destroys the monarchy. The Second World War punishes the madness of the dictator and destroys the city. It lays in pieces, broken into two. Nowhere else in the world do capitalism and communism collide so blatantly than at this divide between the two global systems brought forth by the creation of two German states in 1949. The Wall is built in 1961. It takes until 1989 before it is torn down again. The world is astonished and cries tears of joy –

Berlin without its death corridor. Today, reunited and with the insignia of capital and seat of government, the people seek new paths. Into Europe, towards the East. Not an easy journey for sure, but rather an exciting one!

VICTORY COLUMN (SIEGESSÄULE)

Gilded canons are reminiscent of the supposed glorious Prussian era; of the battles fought in the campaigns against Denmark, Austria and France between 1864 and 1871. The 69 metre high column designed by J. H. Strack in the heart of the Tiergarten Park stands out for all to see at the centre of the Great Star in the direct vicinity of the new Federal President's residence. F. Drake sculpted the gilded figure, 37 tonnes in weight, which represents Victoria, the Goddess of Victory, but which people have lovingly referred to as "Golden Elsie" for time immemorial.

◁ *Debis Building · Potsdam Square*   *Marlene Dietrich Square · "Daimler City" Potsdam Square* ▽

△ *Victory Column*

Reichstag Building, Plenary Hall ▽

REICHSTAG BUILDING (REICHSTAGSGEBÄUDE)

Paul Wallot completed the Reichstag Building in 1894, which was originally intended to house the members of parliament elected by secret ballot. The parliamentary system collapsed under the Weimar Republic as a result of the general intolerance of the bourgeois parties. The general assembly hall was destroyed by arsonists in 1933. Soldiers of the Red Army hoisted the Hammer and Sickle in 1945. In autumn 1999 fifty years had passed before a parliament, this time the German Bundestag, was once more able to reside in the building redesigned by Sir Norman Forster.

BRANDENBURG GATE (BRANDENBURGER TOR)

Europe's symbolic gate is the only building to appear on three German euro coins. This too underlines the significance of the mighty trademark: the western entrance gate to the metropolis. Commissioned by "Beautiful Wilhelmina", the voluptuous mistress of Frederick William II, King of Prussia, C. G. Langhans created the ensemble from 1788 to 1791 in celebration of the Hellenistic culture. J.G. Schadow crowned it with his "Quadriga", which burnt out in May 1945. "New" horses have decorated the portal since 1958.

Brandenburg Gate ▽

Reichstag Building ▽

UNTER DEN LINDEN

Pariser Platz, an exact square 144 metres in length, opens up the view to a reborn Berlin as seat of government and capital. Mammon, Muses and millionaires all reside here only too demonstratively. Banks, Embassies of France and the USA, the Academy of Arts and the VIPs all of whom put their heads to pillow in the legendary *Hotel Adlon*. The sumptuous refuge of Lorenz Adlon has been the very first address amongst the noble hotels since 1907. Reopened in the summer of 1997, the hotel has now confirmed its justified claim of belonging to one of the best twelve hotels in the world. The avenue "Unter den Linden" ("Under the Lime Trees") starts here, ending one and a half kilometres further east at the *Schloßbrücke*. For the people of Berlin, the lime trees symbolise the start of well-conceived urban planning. The Great Elector ordered them to be planted in 1647 at the end of the Thirty Years' War. An avenue of a thousand trees, standing six rows deep: nut trees and lime trees. In the eighteenth century, subsidies from the King assisted the building of noble villas. Since the boom experienced during the period of promoterism, commercial buil-

▽ *Unter den Linden · Monument of Frederick the Great, Mounted on Horse*

dings and the Berlin headquarters of corporate groups, car manufacturers, embassies (Russia, Hungary, Poland, Saudi Arabia) and the like have lined this special avenue. The German Bundestag moved its headquarters and some of the MP offices here. ZDF, the German state television company, now also has its capital studio here. The world renown coffee shop of the Viennese confectioner J. G. Kranzler was located at the cross-roads to the Friedrichstraße from 1825 to 1944. Kranzler was the first to receive a royal permit to serve ice cream and cake to his regular guests – young officers – in the open air. The gourmet temples of Dressel and Hiller, serving frogs legs and quail eggs, were to be found opposite his coffee shop. The traffic thoroughfare, lit by electric street lanterns since 1888, was already so busy by the turn of the century that four traffic policemen had to regulate traffic on the Friedrichstraße. The building of the **state library** (the largest glass dome in the city covered its reading room until 1944) is home to objects of inestimable value such the original score of Beethoven's IXth symphony along with some 4 million books. The **Humboldt University**, the **Neue Wache** and the

Pariser Platz · Hotel Adlon ▽

Zeughaus are located on the same side of the road facing east. On the opposite side is the ***Crown Prince's Palace (Kronprinzenpalais)***, the ***Princess' Palace (Prinzessinenpalais)***, ***German State Opera*** and ***"Kommode"***. The 'Linden' as the people of Berlin refer to their prestigious avenue, has become the place for the Greats in their time. During his only stay in Berlin in May 1778, Goethe stayed at the "Gasthaus zum Russischen Hof" with a view of the magnificent avenue. Schiller did the same thing in 1804. Heinrich Heine provides the wittiest reflections of bourgeois pride and philistine thinking, genius and noblesse in many articles he wrote starting in 1822. As a young deputy, Bismarck lived in 'Unter den Linden'. As a hotel guest he wrote a rather rebellious letter to his King, which flouted protocol and brought the monarch's attention to the young nobleman from the Elbe for the first time. An innovation of city history also originated from the Linden. The first normal clock was installed above the portal of the Academy of Sciences in 1787 by C. Möllinger which the verger of all church clocks was required to follow.

▽ *Unter den Linden · Neue Wache*

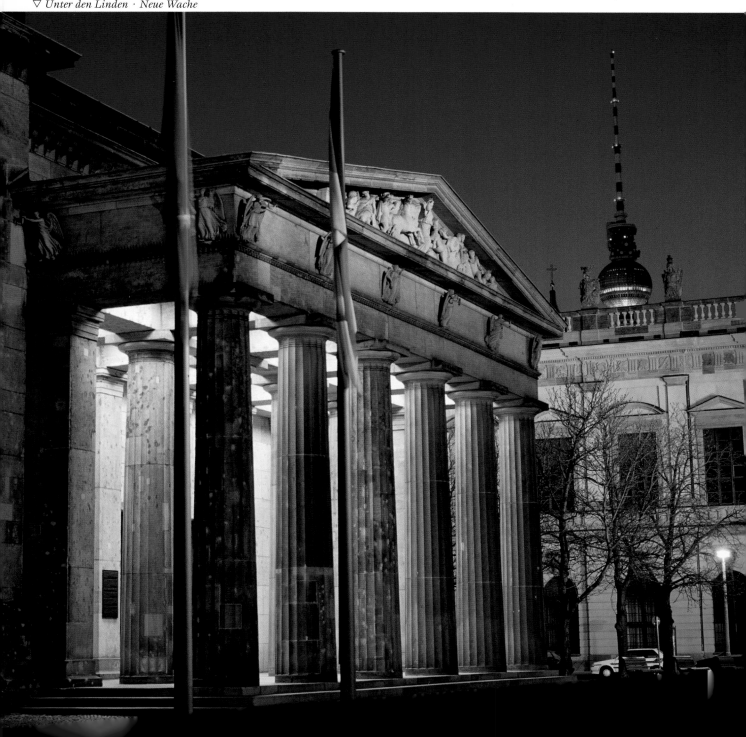

△ *Crown Prince's Palace*   △ *Opera Café*   *Schloßbrücke, Berlin Cathedral, Television Tower* ▽

IN AND AROUND THE POTSDAM SQUARE (POTSDAMER PLATZ)

Only rubble remained of the busiest squares on the continent, the heart of economic life in the Swinging Twenties. The historic Weinhaus Huth was the only building left. The first plans were made in the summer of 1989; building started in 1991 and has been in progress ever since – for around five billion euros. The breathtaking ensemble with its snug skyscrapers boldly presenting itself in a form never before witnessed in Berlin also symbolises the spirit of the Berlin Republic. The mega city 2000. Cool, calculating and mercurial. Debis and Sony rule their business empires from here. High-tech jobs, futuristic ambience, transparent architecture (Renzo Piano and Helmut Jahn), perfect traffic connections by regional, local and underground trains, trams and underground road tunnels mix together in the melting pot that is Berlin. The **Arcades** provide the ultimate shopping experience. Bistros and casinos, restaurants and cinemas (the **IMAX** is one of the most highly frequented cinemas in Europe), the Grand Hyatt and the **Musical Theatre** all rub shoulders with each other.

▽ *View from the Landwehrkanal towards the Debis Building on the Potsdam Square*

△ Sony-Center

Galeries Lafayette · Friedrichstraße ▽

△ *Friedrichstraße*   ▽ *"Planet Hollywood"*   △ *Potsdamer-Platz-Arkaden*   ▽ *Quartier 206/Friedrichstadtpassagen*

FRIEDRICHSTRASSE

The exact link between the north and south of the city between Oranienburger Tor and Hallesche Tor: a lively boulevard – subculture around Tacheles, showtime in the *Friedrichstadtpalast*, Brecht cult following in the *Berliner Ensemble*. A shopper's paradise to the south of the hyper-modern regional and local train station: *Dussmann's Kulturkaufhaus*, *Lafayette* on the other side of 'Linden' and the *Quartier 206*. The Friedrichstraße attracts young people in the evening too with its boutiques, bars and pubs. *"Planet Hollywood"* is a known meeting place with high flirt factor.

POLICEMEN'S MARKET

(GENDARMENMARKT) Designed by Frederick II around 1740, home to many great minds, including E. T. A. Hoffmann. In the centre K. F. Schinkels *"Schauspielhaus"* (Theatre) which nowadays is primarily used as a concert hall. Two remarkable permanent exhibitions are now housed in the towers of the *German* (left of the Schiller Monument) and the *French Cathedral*: "Questions of German History" and "The Hugenots in Berlin". Opposite is the building of the "Seehandlung", the first commodity futures market and foreign trade bank in Prussia.

Gendarmenmarkt · German Cathedral ▽

△▽ *Hackesche Höfe*

HACKESCHE HÖFE

Long a Mecca for the predominantly young night-owls and early morning birds. Built originally around 1900 as a goods warehouse and offices in the colourful bricks typically found in Hamburg, the widespread area was painstakingly restored with great attention to detail soon after the political changes owing to its relatively intact condition: off stages, cinemas, cabarets, galleries, bits and bobs, wine shops and bars of all types have settled here. The "Chamäleon" has been known for years as a revue house with the very best reputation.

RED TOWN HALL
(ROTES RATHAUS)

The name originates from the colour of the stone: the light red building material for the terracotta was procured from a village called Wassersuppe near Rathenow. Built by H. F. Waesemann between 1861 and 1870 with four wings – some 100 metres square. The 97 m high tower – not home to the bell of freedom which is in Schöneberg – symbolises Tuscan stylistic elements. Seat of the Governing Town Mayor. Meeting halls and state rooms are generally open to the public on week-days.

Red Town Hall ▽

ST. NICHOLAS' QUARTER (NIKOLAIVIERTEL)

Make new in old – with this in mind the East Berlin municipal council created a quarter as never seen before in 1987 for Berlin's 750th anniversary in the heart of the "East German capital" as it was then. Prefabricated slab buildings at the back, sandstone facades at the front: 800 flats, shops, hospitality. Right in the middle of the St. Nicholas' Quarter is the "Nußbaum" (The Nut Tree). Heinrich Zilles' regular pub, often drawn by him. This too is a decorative new building. The original "Nußbaum" was some-where completely different, on the Fischerinsel (Fishermen's Island). Nevertheless, the small intact quarter behind the Red Town Hall does have flair. It is the right mix that does it: the **"Ephraim-Palais"** (G. E. Lessing lived here from 1752 to 1755), pubs such as the "Gerichtslaube", "Zur Rippe" or the "Paddenwirt" and tiny shops. Patios to see and sun-bathe on, no cars; the early classicist town house of the Knoblauch family (of 1760) is now a memorial together with a small wine house. Another museum is nearby which centres on hamp

◁ *St. Nicholas' Quarter · St. Nicholas' Church and St. George Monument*

St. Nicholas' Quarter ▽

ALEXANDER SQUARE (ALEXANDERPLATZ)

Once a bullock market, and then renamed in honour of Tsar Alexander in 1805. During the twenties it was Europe's liveliest thoroughfare with five levels. A. Döblin and his hero Franz Biberkopf gave it a place in literary history. Largely devastated during the war. Then disputed model socialist architecture. Located between the local train station (S-Bahnhof) and the Forum Hotel (with the highest cocktail bar in Germany) is "Alex" with the **world clock** and the Bauhaus buildings of Alexander and Berolina (Architect: P. Behrens). Still a top place to be.

TELEVISION TOWER (FERNSEHTURM)

365 m high, only the television tower in Moscow makes the "telescopic asparagus" look small. The idea of building the giant (in swamps!) originated from the GDR's chief architect H. Henselmann. Where narrow alleys once were there is now an open space across the 'Neptune Fountain' (by R. Begas) to the shell of the Palace of the Republic. Private TV companies broadcast their programmes from this television tower (owned by Telekom). The revolving restaurant (200 m high) is the best seat in the city.

◁ *Alexander Square with world clock*   *Television Tower, Red Town Hall, St. Nicholas' Church* ▽

IN AND AROUND
THE KURFÜRSTENDAMM

It used to be a bridlepath leading Elector Joachim Hektor westwards from the Tiergarten Park to his hunting fields and Grunewald hunting lodge around 1550. Only during Bismarck's time did urban planners turn it into a straight and broad riding path modelled on the Parisian Champs-Elysées. The great boom began with the turbulent Gründerzeit from 1875 and around the turn of the century when the Prussian moneyed nobility settled away from the old centre before the gates of the city in fine palaces and noble villas in Grunewald. The logical consequence: far-sighted property speculators took possession of the land along the cobbled road which was over 50 metres wide to Halensee and also created the best bourgeois houses here. In the Golden Twenties this fine quarter was given the name "The New West". Cafés, cinemas, theatres, fashion shops and night bars sprang up here. The famous comedian cabarets had their home here. But it was only at the end of the war and the Berlin Blockade (1948/1949) that the Kürfürstendamm became the actual main traffic route of the western part of the divided city. The bou-

▽ *Memorial Church*

△ *Europe Centre, water clock*

▽ *Europe Centre, "Tiffany's"*

Europe Centre △

levard curiously starts with house number 11 direct-
ly at the Breitscheidplatz; the first section of the
"Kudamm" south of the *Zoological Gardens* is called Budapester Straße as a loyal gesture to the once
influential Hungarian emigrants. The first landmark
of the boulevard is the *Europe Centre* (architect
H. Pepper) opened in 1965 with the Hotel Palace and
its noble boutiques and international bistros. The
indestructible cabaretists, the "Stachelschweine"
(The Porcupines), reside in the basement. The nearby Kranzler corner on Joachimsthaler Straße is an
incessantly throbbing hubbub, and has been recently
embedded into the new shining business building
designed by the architects Murphy & Jahn, Chicago;
opposite is a hypermodern C&A fashion department
store. There are several luxury hotels within view of
this cross-roads. The most famous is the Bristol Hotel
Kempinski. Lined by wide pavements and leafy trees
along a length of three and a half kilometres with
front gardens too numerous to mention. Restaurants
to suit every taste (and pocket); a place to stroll along
on hot and cooler days for young and old. It goes
without saying that flats on the Kudamm in magnificent old buildings decorated with stucco from the

▽ *Berlin sculpture*

Kürfürstendamm with Memorial Church ▷

△ Bellevue Palace

Charlottenburg Palace, Porcelain Cabinet ▽

English country gardens) served as a feudal tea house of the monarchs. It contains a noteworthy porcelain collection from the Berlin potteries W. C. Wegely and J. E. Gotzkowsky. A little further up the River Spree towards the east is the **Bellevue Palace**, official residence of the Federal President. After R. v. Weizsäcker resolved to conduct his official business from Berlin in 1991, the administration of the highest state office is located in the so-called 'presidential egg' since the government moved in summer 1999. P. D. Boumann built a three-wing palace for Prince Ferdinand (youngest brother of Frederick II) on the site where in the seventeenth century a dairy provided the monarch's court with milk, butter and cheese. Langhans designed the oval room. After restoration work following considerable damage during the war, T. Heuß was the first Federal President to move into the repaired house. Monbijou Palace, which similarly stood near the Spree and served Queen Elisabeth, wife of Frederick II, was torn down, however. Three significant feudal buildings remain in the eastern part of the city: **Niederschönhausen Palace** in Pankow (Göthe), as government guest house during GDR times. **Friedrichsfelde Palace** in

Friedrichsfelde Palace ▽

Lichtenberg am Tierpark was built around 1700 by Nering as a residence for the Dutch Admiral B. v. Raulé. **Köpenick Palace**, the oldest state building in Berlin, is built on the foundations of a Slav fortress dating back to the eighth century. It was restored by Nering around 1690 as a water palace. Worth seeing today: magnificent fireplaces and an Augsburg silver collection. In 1825 K. F. Schinkel designed the **Tegel Palace** for the Humboldt family. The **summer residence** on the Peacock Island (built in 1795 by J. G. Brendel as a love nest for Frederick William II and his mistress Wilhemina) and **Kleinglienicke Palace**

are two interesting buildings located on the western edge of the city. Schinkel and L. Persius created a classic ensemble of unsurpassable stylistic purity here.

◁ *Residence on Peacock Island*

Kleinglienicke Palace ▽

MEMORIAL CHURCH (GEDÄCHTNISKIRCHE)

As one of the most unusual building ensembles in post-war Berlin, the Kaiser William Memorial Church unifies contradictory elements which reflect fragments of Prussian history in the twentieth century: majestic ostentation and the scars of total defeat side by side. William II had the Church (architect: F. Schwechten) inaugurated in 1895 in memory of his grandfather Kaiser William I. The oversized mosaics in the tower, the "Prince Freeze" are reminiscent of the old Zeitgeist. The nave fell to bombs in 1943. E. Eiermann won the architectural competition in 1957 and created a church which is divided into three parts: the fragments of the ruin, the hexagonal campanile and the octagonal prayer house. The inside of the church, with purple, turquoise and azure-coloured glass windows by G. Loire, create a calm oasis of seclusion despite the city noise outside. The figure of Christ the redeemer suspended above the stone altar by K. Hemmeter shines in ever new fascinating nuances created by distorted daylight.

▽ *Memorial Church, mosaics in the old tower; centre photo from left to right: Kaiser William I., Frederick III, William II*

△ *Memorial Church, altar and cross*

Memorial Church, old tower/memorial hall ▽

BERLIN CATHEDRAL
(BERLINER DOM)

In keeping with the intention of its architect, the Berlin Cathedral was to lift the capital of the new kingdom to the heights of the "Rome of the Protestants". The dome, with its four turrets and the facade in the style of the Italian High Renaissance, was intended to give Protestant Christians a "German St. Peter's", the epitome of their belief. In the face of great resistance Kaiser William II had Schinkel's house of God border an ornamental garden. The new building by J. C. Raschdorff (built 1894–1905) opposite the palace provided the Hohenzollerns with room for more than 2000 worshippers. Despite serious damage during the war, the East German government kept the cathedral ruin and supported the expensive restoration of the copper roof structure. The painstaking restoration of nave and prince's crypt was started after 1990. Marble statues, windows and gold-shining mosaics match the originals destroyed in the war down to the last detail. The Cathedral is frequently used for concerts owing to its good acoustic qualities.

▽ *Berlin Cathedral*

Berlin Cathedral · Main Altar ▷

ST. MARY'S CHURCH
(MARIENKIRCHE)

It is first mentioned in 1294 when at that time the church was a single-nave building made of field stones. The house of God was the centre of the "new town" located outside the gates of the original Berlin. In 1340 it was engulfed by fire and as from 1420 restored in stages and extended to a three-nave church. Work was started on the "Dance of Death", a fresco two metres in height and 22 metres in length in the north tower in 1485 and is one of the oldest art treasures of the city.

▽ *St. Mary's Church*

ST. NICHOLAS' CHURCH (NIKOLAIKIRCHE)

Archaeological excavations discovered foundations from Roman times beneath St. Nicholas' Church. After the Christians settled here their Church grew with them as from 1230. This made St. Nicholas' the first sacramental building of the city and it has remained its most significant to this very day. The fortified turret from this age is Berlin's oldest building. The Church has been restored and changed for over 500 years. It was badly damaged during the Second World War and has been undergoing reconstruction since 1982 (according to drawings from 1876).

St. Nicholas' Church ▽

St. Hedwig's Cathedral ▽

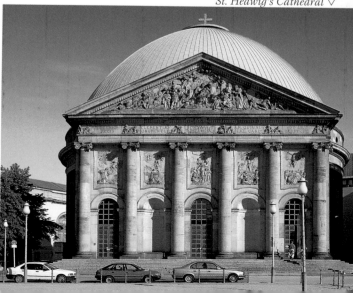

ST. HEDWIG'S CATHEDRAL

(ST.-HEDWIGS-KATHEDRALE) After the conquest of Silesia King Federick II gave his court architect G. W. von Knobelsdorff the order to build the new subjects in Prussia their own cathedral which was named after the patron saint of Silesian miners, Saint Hedwig. The enlightened monarch thus created the first Roman Catholic church in Brandenburg. Started in 1747, the church was built in the style of the Roman Pantheon. It was fully burnt down in 1943 and rebuilt in the period 1952 to 1963. It is now the seat of the Cardinal and the Archbishop of Berlin.

GERMAN AND FRENCH CATHEDRAL

The buildings were given the misleading name "cathedral" from the French "dôme" which simply means "dome" and not cathedral. Frederick II created a piazza in Roman style on which the impressive Schauspielhaus (theatre) is flanked by two sacral monuments. The two identical towers (1780 to 1785 by K. Gontard and G.C. Unger) decorate the centres of the Hugenot (French) and Protestant (German) church.

German and French Cathedral ▽

FRIEDRICH WERDER CHURCH (FRIEDRICH-WERDERSCHE KIRCHE)

Around 1825 Prussia's most prominent architect K. F. Schinkel carried out the order from the King to turn a tumbledown church into a neo-gothic building. Designed in brick, the structure built in the style of the English chapel influenced the sacral style of North Germany through to the end of the nineteenth century. Badly damaged in the war, Schinkel's building was restored from 1982 to 1987. It now serves as a memorial and as a museum for sculptures from the period of classicism.

▽ *Friedrich Werder Church*

NEW SYNAGOGUE (NEUE SYNAGOGE)

F. A. Stüler, a Christian, completed the expensive Jewish temple in Germany. Building commenced in 1859 as a main synagogue to provide room for 3200 people; 35000 Jews lived in Berlin at this time. A flourishing community life developed on the Oranienburger Straße in the largest Jewish centre of the German Reich. The building was set on fire by the SA during the "Kristallnacht" (9 November 1938) and the ruin bombed in 1943. Since 1995 the Moorish golden dome shines for all to see over the former Jewish quarter.

New Synagogue ▷

MUSEUM ISLAND

King Frederick William III and his son, Frederick William IV characterise a long stretch of Prussian history in which the enlightened monarchs saw themselves as patrons in their city. At the end of the Wars of Liberation and the end of the Napoleonic Era two elementary factors influenced the monarchy in the flourishing city: the will to raise Prussia to a bastion of the beaux arts and the development of a remarkably broad strata of the population which felt committed to the spirit of the Antiquity. From 1824 onwards the **Altes Museum (Old Museum)**, built on flattened swampland between the Spree and Kupfergraben, represented the core of an ensemble conceived on a large scale. This building was designed by K. F. Schinkel with 18 ionistic columns in the style of a classic Hellenistic temple. It is Berlin's oldest museum complex. In front of it is the "Soup Dish" created by C. G. Cantian in 1829 – a granite dish weighing some 80 tonnes and carved from a foundling stone in the Rauen Hills. A cultural Mecca has since developed along the top edge of the ornamental gardens. Back in 1841 a Cabinet Order of the King decreed that the area was "a district devoted to

▽ *Museum Island*

art and the science of Antiquity". The **Neues Museum (New Museum)** was completed in 1855, followed two decades later by the **National Gallery**. The Kaiser Frederick Museum (today's **Bode Museum**) and finally the **Pergamon Museum** (started 1909) followed during the reign of Kaiser William II. As a result of war and post-war confusion, it was only completed in 1930. Wilhelm Bode (born 1845), as director general of all Prussian museums, did not live to see the reconstructed Pergamon Alter opened to the public. Bode died in 1929. The step altar brought to the Pergamon

Museum am Kupfergraben (built by A. Messel and consciously modelled on the style of the Brandenburg Gate) from Asia Minor in 1902 is one of the most significant works of art in Europe and is viewed to be a miracle of Antiquity. Created around 170 B.C., it was an ostentatious shrine for Zeus and Athena.

Pergamon Altar ▽

Pergamon Museum ▽

△ Altes Museum

Flute concert of Frederick II (Adolf Menzel) ▽

MUSEUMS

The division of the city in autumn 1948 and the building of the Wall in 1961 were the reasons why cultural policy developed along two strictly different tracks and why a new museum landscape constantly grew in the western part of Berlin. Back in 1955, for example, the decision was made to transfer a complex to the Foundation of Prussian Culture in Dahlem which clearly broke away from the traditional museums. The core of the Asian Museum (largely used only as a depository) built by B. Paul in 1914–1923 was supplemented by the three-winged building constructed by G. Grimmek between 1964 and 1973. In addition to the extensive **Museum of German Folklore**, and the **Copper Engraving Cabinet**, the ensemble also includes the **Sculpture Gallery** and the **Art Gallery**. In 1996 these moved to the **Kulturforum** on Kemper Square near the Philharmonic. This also includes the **New National Gallery** (L. Mies v. d. Rohe), the **Musical Instruments Museum** (H. Scharoun) and the **Crafts Gallery** (R. Gutbrod). The Hamburg train station is one quarter of an hour away (redesigned by J. P. Kleihues) as **Museum of Contemporary Art** in

Kulturforum ▽

Hamburg train station, Museum of Contemporary Art ▽

which the Berlin patron Erich Marx presents his collection. Despite war damage, the existing masterpieces from the realms of painting, sculpture and Greco-Roman Antiquity have been kept in the historical centre of the eastern part of the city since 1950 – on the museum island and in the oldest state building Unter den Linden, namely the **Zeughaus** (N. F. Blondel/A. Schlüter) which served the GDR as a museum of German history. It is now the **German Museum of History**. It is currently being restored and supplemented with a futuristic glass dome (works are temporarily kept in the Crown Prince's Palace opposite). Over one thousand exhibits which were stored in mines in Hesse came back to Berlin (West) in 1957 – including without question the most famous treasure: the bust of Nofretete. Excavated in Tell-el-Amarna in 1912. The Queen was the wife of Pharaoh Echnaton whose bust, together with an ebony bust of Teje, Echnaton's mother, is to be found in the extensive collection. Still currently in Charlottenburg Palace, exhibited in one of the two classic domed houses by F. A. Stüler (around 1850) (**Egyptian Museum**; it will return to the New Museum on the Museum Island in the sum-

▽ *Egyptian Museum, Nofretete around 1350 B.C.*

△ *Zeughaus, German History Museum*

Berggruen collection (formerly Museum of Antiquity) ▽

△ *Chamber Music Hall*

Concert in the Schauspielhaus ▽

around him were the nobility of the state; the low ranks were banned to the upper and lower circles. Theatre had to wait longer for recognition in Prussia than in Paris or Vienna. Only with the arrival of A. W. Iffland in 1796 as director of the National Theatre were modern and moving dramas from Goethe and Schiller included in the programme, attracting Germany's best actors. By contrast, the Unter den Linden Opera House fell into crisis. The building burned down almost completely in 1843 and in 1941 and was lovingly restored with great attention to detail in 1987. Under the leadership of D. Barenboim it is now Europe's top address, quite able to hold its own with the Milan Scala, the Dresdner Semper Opera and the Vienna State Opera. The **German Opera House of Berlin** on the Bismarckstraße, the **Comical Opera House** (under H. Kupfer) in the Behrenstraße and the **Small Opera House** which is not afraid to experiment in Neukölln all enjoy a high reputation. This also applies to the Berlin Philharmonic which has had only five directors since 1887: v. Bülow, A. Nikisch, W. Furtwängler, H. v. Karajan and C. Abbado (since 1989). The most important theatres compete with

Schauspielhaus on the Policemen's Market (Gendarmenmarkt) ▽

HOUSE OF WORLD CULTURES (HAUS DER KULTUREN DER WELT)

Located on the shore of the River Spree, half way between the Bellevue Palace, the residence of the Federal President, and the new Chancellery. Built in 1957 as a donation from the citizens of the USA (H. Stubbins). Berlin's first congress hall was quickly christened the "Pregnant Oyster" owing to its usual shape. Serious construction faults which went unnoticed led to the roof collapsing in 1980, killing several people. Re-opened in 1987. Nowadays used as a meeting place for multicultural activities.

ICC AND EXHIBITION CENTRE (MESSE)

The International Congress Center (U. Schüler-Witte and R. Schüler) was built in the period 1973 to 1979 near to the radio tower and exhibition grounds to replace the congress hall which soon became too small. 20,000 people can meet simultaneously in 90 rooms of different sizes in the futuristic complex. Not including the Tempelhof Airport, the ICC, 320 metres long and 80 metres wide, has 800 000 square metres, making it the biggest building in the city.

▽ *Olympic Stadium*

▽ *House of World Cultures (former Congress Hall)*

ICC/Exhibition Centre

Radio Tower ▽

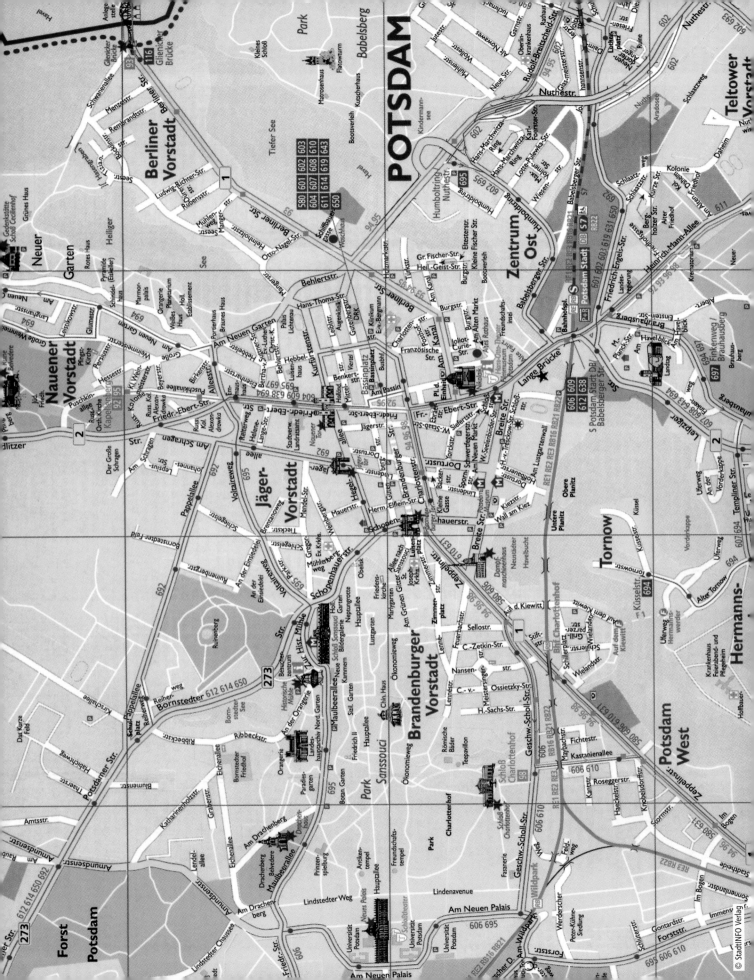

PALACE AND SANSSOUCI PARK

The word "sans souci" means without worries. G. W. v. Knobelsdorff, King Frederick II's architect who designed the "modest house on the vineyard" according to the monarch's ideas, had restored the country residence "Kummerfrei" in Silesia years before. It can therefore be assumed that the name originated from here. Knobelsdorff had to put up with ungracious criticism from the King during construction who sketched the facade in his own hand. The monarch had a "vigne" in mind, i.e. a winegrowers house. Today, following extensive renovation in and around

Sanssouci, one of the most significant closed ensembles in the world has been excellently restored. The monarch's last wish to be buried on the patio next to his dogs was also respected. The uniqueness is not only rooted in the francophile taste of the monarch, but also in the unassuming elegance which characterised the aesthete. Men such as Voltaire and Casanova visited his court. His successors, such as the italophile Frederick William IV, whose ideal building style was reminiscent of Venetian masters, lend the landscape around Potsdam its own very special character even today. And in Victoria, the wife of

▽ *Sanssouci Palace*

Kaiser Frederick III, even a committed "green" moved in. The daughter of Queen Victoria managed her land according to ecological principles. The change also becomes noticeable during an extended walk through Sanssouci: Whilst Old Fritz had created a purely private place for himself and his entourage ("women and priests" were not allowed in, his majesty's greyhounds wore collars of silver) and enjoyed the flair of unique surroundings in his golden Tea House which were reserved for him alone as the absolute ruler over his people, the following Prussian Kings added their own touch. On the one hand they retreated into the world of Roman Antiquity such as Frederick William IV, whilst almost at the same time the Babelsberg Palace was built for his younger brother William I (who was later to become German Kaiser) in a Norman castle style. His grandson, Kaiser William II, used the area in front of the New Palais for military parades.

Sanssouci Palace, Concert Room ▽

Sanssouci Park △ *Chinese Tea House* ▽ *New Palais*   *Chinese Tea House, Mandarin* △

POTSDAM · CECILIENHOF PALACE IN THE NEW GARDEN

Kaiser William's son, the crown prince, built a seemingly modest – by standards at that time – manor house of half timber in an English cottage style in the form of the Cecilienhof Palace (built between 1914 and 1917) on the shore of the Heiligen See. With the exception of the two-storey hall (with its famous Danzig guild staircase) the rooms are all low and tastefully decorated. The Three Powers met in the Cecilienhof in the summer of 1945 during the Potsdam Conference.

POTSDAM

The capital of the federal state of Brandenburg, it was viewed to be the Venice of the March; river arms, bridges, palaces. A quiet Arcadia of noble families in Prussia with close military connections. Established one thousand years ago as a fishing village, it became the headquarters of the powerful state during the later life of Frederick the Great. Severe Anglo-American bomb attacks destroyed the city centre in 1944. The palace was burned down. Only later did the East German regime put a stop to the devastating clearance.

◁◁ *Potsdam · Cecilienhof Palace in the New Garden*

Potsdam, Harbour with St. Nicholas' Church ▽